A Family Well-Ordered

or

An essay to render parents and children happy in one another, handling two very important cases

1. What are the duties to be done by pious parents to promote piety in their children?

2. What are the duties that must be paid by children to their parents that they may obtain the blessings of the dutiful?

by
Cotton Mather

Edited by Dr. Don Kistler

Soli Deo Gloria Publications
. . . for instruction in righteousness . . .

Soli Deo Gloria Publications
P. O. Box 451, Morgan, PA 15064
(412) 221-1901/FAX 221-1902
www.SDGbooks.com

*

*

ISBN 1-57358-126-7

The Duties of Parents to their Children

"I know him, that he will command his children, and his household after him, and they shall keep the way of the Lord." Genesis 18:19

As the great God, who at the beginning said, "Let us make man after our image," has made man a sociable creature, so it is evident that families are the nurseries of all societies. And the first combinations of mankind, well-ordered families, naturally produce a good order in other societies. When families are under an ill discipline, all other societies, being ill-disciplined as a result, will feel that error in the first concoction. To serve the families of our neighborhood will be a service to all our interests. Every serious Christian is concerned to be serviceable in the world. And many a serious Christian is concerned because he sees himself to be furnished with no more opportunities to be serviceable.

But are you not a member of some family? If that family may by your means, O Christian, become a well-regulated family, in that point you will become serviceable. They who have the government of some family make up no little part of this great assembly. And, sirs, are there any of you who would forfeit that honorable title of all the faithful, "the children of Abraham"? Give your attention, you children of Abraham, while I set before you the example of your father for your imitation.

Our glorious Lord Messiah is here going to communicate unto Abraham some of His heavenly counsels. And we have a text before us that assigns a reason for that gracious communication. The reason is the care which this good man would thereupon take to bring up his family in the fear of God. In this text there are some remarkable things, and things that some wise men have often remarked. There was an excellent man, sometimes a preacher of the Lord Jesus Christ in this very place, whose custom it was not only to read a protion of the Scripture before his prayers with his family, but also to infer and apply brief notes out of what he read. He professed that he found none of all his weary studies in divinity so profitable to him as this one, for the rare and rich thoughts which he therein found supplied himself withal. He declared that he looked on it as an accomplishment of this very word, "Shall I hide from Abraham the thing which I do? I know him, that he will command his children and his household."

Moreover, you may here observe a most comfortable connection between "he will" and "they shall." The Lord says, "He will command his children, and they shall keep the way of the Lord." It seems that if everyone who is owner of a family would faithfully command and manage those who belong to him, through the blessing of God they would generally keep his way and his law. I find a famous writer in the church therefore expressing himself thus: "If parents did their duties as they ought, the Word publically preached would not be the ordinary means of regeneration in the church, also outside the church, among infidels. God would so pour out His grace upon the children of his people, and hear prayers for them, and bless endeavors for their holy education, that we would see the promises made good unto our seed."

We will now dismiss these reflections and repair to that grand case which offers itself to us, which is:

What may be done by pious parents to promote the piety and salvation of their children?

The case inquires, what may be done? You'll take it for granted that the answer to it will tell you what should be done. For you'll readily grant that in such an important case as this, all that *may* be done *should* be done.

In this first case, we inquire after what is to be done by pious parents. Other parents will take no due notice of the injunctions that God has laid upon them concerning their children. Parents, if you don't first become pious yourselves, you'll do nothing to purpose to make your children so. Unless you yourselves walk in the way of the Lord, you will be very careless about bringing your children to such a walk. It is not a Cain, nor a Ham, nor any enemy of God who will do anything to make his children become the children of God. In Psalm 34:1, 4, and 11 the psalmist could first say, "I'll bless the Lord," and then, "I sought the Lord," and then, "Come ye children, and I'll teach you the fear of the Lord." O parents, in the name of God, look after your own miserable souls. How should those wretched people do anything for the souls of their children who never did anything for their own?

Also, in this case, we inquire what is to be done by parents for their children. But let it be remembered that our servants are, in some sort, like our children. Our whole household, as well as the childen who are our offspring, are to be taught the way of the Lord. An

Abraham will have his trained servants. We read, concerning a certain person of quality, in 2 Kings 5:13, "His servants came near and spake unto him, and said, 'My father.' " Let not those of my hearers who are without such invaluable blessings of God as children, count themselves unconcerned in our discourse, if they have any servants under them. A considerable part of what is to be done for our children may be done for your servants. And may God make Eliezers of them for you!

Attend now to these counsels of God:

1. Parents, consider the condition of your children, and the loud cry of their condition to you to endeavor their salvation! What an army of powerful thoughts at once now show themselves, to besiege your hearts and subdue them unto a just care for the salvation of your children!

Do you not know that your children have precious and immortal souls within them? They are not all flesh. You who are the parents of their flesh must know that your children have spirits also. You are told in Hebrews 12:9 that God is the Father of them, and in Ecclesiastes 12:7 that God is the Giver of them. The souls of your children must survive their bodies, and are transcendently better, higher, and nobler things than their bodies. Are you solicitous that their bodies be fed? You should be more solicitous that their souls may not be starved, or go without the Bread of Life. Are you solicitous that their bodies may be clothed? You should be more solicitous that their souls may not be naked, or go without the garments of righteousness. Are you loath to have their bodies laboring under infirmities or deformities? You should be much more loath to have their souls pining away in their iniquities.

Man, are your children but the children of swine? If you disregard their souls, truly you call them so! One of the ancients, namely Cyprian, had a pungent comparison for this matter: "Pray, consider, he who minds his child's body more than his soul is like one who, if his child and his dog were both drowning, was solicitous to save his dog and let his child perish in the water." How deaf you are, that you do not hear the loud cry from the souls of your children in your ears: "O my father, my mother, look after me!"

But more than this, don't you know that your children are the children of death, the children of hell, and the children of wrath by nature? Don't you know that from you this nature is derived and conveyed unto them? You must know, parents, that your children are by your means born under the dreadful wrath of God. And if they are not born again before they die, it would have been good for them that they have never been born at all. In Exodus 21:19, the law of equity was that if one man wounds another, he shall cause him to be thoroughly healed. Your children are born with deadly wounds upon their souls, and they may thank you for those wounds. Unjust men, will you now do nothing for their healing? Man, your children are dying of a horrid poison, and it was you who poisoned them. What, will you do nothing for their succour! Your children are thrown into a devouring fire, and it is from you that the fiery vengeance of God has taken hold of them. What, will you do nothing to help them out!

There is a corrupt nature in your children, which is a fountain of all wickedness and confusion. The very pagans were not insensible of this corrupt nature. They called it our "congenite sin" and our "domestic evil."

They cried out with Tertullian, "At the same time as we arrive at the highest light, we continue in all our wickedness." The Jews have been more sensible of this corrupt nature still. They have called it our "evil frame," "the poison of the old serpent," and "the heart of stone." This they understand by the enemy so often mentioned in Scripture. Will not you who are Christians then show your Christianity by sensibly doing what you can so that you children may have a better nature infused into them?

What shall I say? I may say that time would fail me to mention a thousandth part of what might be said. But, in short, is it not a sad thing to be the father of a fool? Alas, man, until your children become regenerate, you are the father of a fool. Your children are but the wild ass's colt! I add, would it not break your heart if your children were in slavery to Turks, Moors, or Indians? Devils are worse than Indians and infidels. Till your children are brought home to God, they are the slaves of devils. In a word, can your heart endure that your children should be banished from the Lord Jesus Christ, and anguishing under the torments of sin among devils in outer darkness throughout eternal ages? Don't call yourself a parent; you are an ostrich! Do not call these young ones the children of your compassions; you have no compassion! I will not say that Zipporah called her husband "a bloody husband." But all the angels in heaven call you "a bloody father" and "a bloody mother." They are astonished at the adamantine hardness of that bloody heart of yours, and those heartstrings that are sinews of iron!

2. Improve the baptism of your children as an obligation and and encouragement unto you, parents, to

endeavor the salvation of your baptized littles ones. Of
your children, you may say, with Jacob in Genesis 33:5,
"These are the children that God hath graciously given
to me." And will you not heartily give back to God those
children once again? Their baptism is to be the sign
and seal of your doing so.

You generally bring your infant children unto the
baptism of the Lord. I suppose you do so because you
are satisfied that the children of believers were in
covenant with God in the days of the Old Testament,
and that the children of believers then had a right unto
the intitial seal of the covenant, and that in the days of
the New Testament they have not lost this privilege.
Well, but when you bring your children to the sacred
baptism, what is it for? Oh, do not let it be done as an
empty formality, as if the baptism of your children were
for nothing but to formally and pompously put a name
upon them. No, but let the serious language of your
souls in this action be that of Hannah in 1 Samuel 1:28:
"I have given this child unto the Lord, as long as he
lives he shall be given unto the Lord."

I find in the private writings of a holy man who died
in this town not more than a year ago that the day before one of his children was to be baptized he spent the
time in giving up himself and his child unto the Lord,
and in taking hold of the covenant for both of them.
He prayed that he might be able the next day, in much
faith, love, and covenant obedience, do it at the baptism of the Lord. On this he wrote, "It is not easy,
though common, to offer a child unto God in baptism."

Sirs, when you have done this for your children, you
have a singular advantage to plead for the fulfillment of

that word upon them from Isaiah 44:3: "I will pour My Spirit upon thy seed, and my blessing upon thy offspring." You may go before the Lord and plead, "Lord, was not the baptismal water poured by Thy command upon my children? Oh, do Thou now pour upon them the heavenly grace which that baptismal water signified." And now, no sooner let those children become able to understand it than you shall make them understand what the design of their baptism was.

Parents, I tell you now that if you let your children grow up without ever telling them *that* and *why* they were baptized into the name of the Lord, you are fearfully guilty of taking the name of the Lord in vain. It was the manner of an excellent minister, upon baptizing a child, to solemnly deliver the child into the hands of the parents with these words, "Here, I charge you to take this child now and bring it up for the Lord Jesus Christ." God from heaven speaks the same words to you, O parents, upon all your baptized children.

And, that you may bring up your children for the Lord Jesus Christ, you must, as soon as you can, let them know that in baptism they were dedicated unto Him. Show them that, when they were baptized, they were listed among the servants and soldiers of the Lord Jesus Christ, and that if they live in rebellion against Him, woe unto them! Show them from Matthew 28:19–20 that, since they are baptized into the name of the Father, the Son, and the Holy Spirit, they must observe all things whatsoever that the Lord Jesus Christ has commanded them to do. Show them from Romans 6:4 that, since they are baptized, they are buried with Christ in baptism, and must live no longer in sin, but are dead unto all the vanities of the world. Show them from

Galatians 3:27 that, since they are baptized, they have put on Christ and must follow His example, and be as He was in the world. Show them from 1 Peter 3:21 that, being baptized, they must now make the answer of a good conscience to all the proposals of the New Covenant.

God propounds to your baptized children, "Shall My Christ be yours, and will you be His?" To this they must conscientiously answer, "Lord, with all my heart!"

Put this very solemnly to your children, "My child, shall God the Father be your Father? Shall God the Son be your Savior? Shall God the Spirit be your Sanctifier? And are you willing to be the servant of that one God, who is Father, Son, and Spirit?" Do not leave them until their little hearts are conquered unto that for which they have been baptized. It has been the judgment of some judicious men that, if infant baptism were more improved, it would be less disputed. Oh, that it were thus improved!

3. Instruct your children in the great matters of salvation. O parents, don't let them die without instruction!

There is indeed an instruction in civil matters which we owe to our children. It is very pleasing to our Lord Jesus Christ that our children should be well-informed with, and well-informed in, the rules of civility, and not be left as clownish, sottish, and ill-bred sorts of creatures. An unmannerly brood is a dishonor to religion. There are many points of a good education that we should bestow upon our children. They should read, write, cypher, and be put into some agreeable callings. And not only our sons, but our daughters also should be taught such things as will later make them useful in their places. There is a little foundation of religion laid in such an education.

But besides and beyond all this, there is an instruction in divine matters which our children are to be-made partakers of. Parents, instruct your children in the articles of religion, and acquaint them with God, Christ, the mysteries of the gospel, and the doctrine and methods of the great salvation. It was so required in Psalm 78:5–7: "He commanded our fathers to make known to their children that the generation to come might know who should arise and declare them to their children, that they might set their hope in God, and keep His commandments." It was required in Ephesians 6:4: "Fathers, bring up your children in the nurture and admonition of the Lord." Would you have your children to be wise and good? I do not know why you should expect it unless you take an abundance of pains by your instruction to make them so.

There was a wise and a good son who gave that account as to how he became what he was in Proverbs 4:3–4: "I was my father's son, and he taught me." Oh, begin early to tell your children who their Maker is and who their Savior is, what they are themselves, and what is likely to become of them. By no means let them lack that advantage found in 2 Timothy 3:15: "From a child thou hast known the Holy Scriptures, which are able to make thee wise unto salvation."

Cause them to look into their Bibles, and here and there single out some special pretenses from those oracles of heaven for them to get into their memories. And for the better management of their instruction, there are two handles especially to be laid hold upon: the first is a proper catechism, and the other is the public ministry. Be sure that they learn their catechism perfectly. But do not content yourselves with hearing them say rotely the answers in their catechism. Question them very distinctly over again about every clause in the answers. Bring all to lie so plainly before them that by their saying only "yes" or "no" you may perceive that the sense of the truth has entered into their souls.

And what they hear in the evangelical ministry, do you apply it unto them after they come home? Confer with them familiarly about the things that have been handled in the ministry of the Word. Go over one thing after another with them till you see that they have gotten clear ideas of them. Then put this unto them: "Are you not now to avoid such a thing, or to perform such a thing? And must you not now make such and such a prayer unto God?" And then bid them to go and do accordingly.

Hence also it would be very desirable that you watch all opportunities to instill your instructions into the souls of your little folks. They are narrow-mouthed vessels, and things must be instilled into them drop after drop. It was required in Deuteronomy 6:6–7: "The words which I command thee, thou shalt teach them diligently unto thy children, and shalt talk of them when thou sittest in thine house, and when thou walkest by the way, and when thou liest down, and when thou risest up." How often in a week do we divert ourselves with our children in our houses? There they stand before us. There is nothing to hinder our saying some very profitable thing for them to think upon. Can you let fall nothing upon them that is worth their while to think upon? What! Nothing of God, of Christ, of another world, of their own souls, of the sins that may endanger them, and of the ways which they may take to be happy? Doubtless you may say *something!*

Who can tell? It may be that, after you have gone to behold the face of the Lord Jesus Christ in glory, your children will remember hundreds of profitable instruction that you have given them, and live upon that instruction you have given them when you are dead.

With two strokes I will clench this advice. The one is from Proverbs 22:6: "Train up a child in the way he should go, and when he is old he will not depart from it." The other is from Proverbs 17:25: "A foolish son is a grief to his father, and a bitterness to her that bare him."

4. Parents, with a sweet authority over your children, rebuke them for and restrain them from everything that may prove prejudicial to their salvation.

Sirs, you can do little for the welfare of your children once you have lost your authority over them. Would you bring your children to the fear of God? Your character, then, must be that mentioned in 1 Timothy 3:4: "One that ruleth well his own house, having his children in subjection with all gravity." Don't allow them, by your lightness, weakness, and folly, to trample upon you; but keep up so much authority that your word may be a law unto them. Nevertheless, do not let your authority be strained with such harshness and fierceness as may discourage your children. To treat our children like slaves, and with such rigor that they shall always tremble and abhor the idea of coming into our presence, is very unlike our heavenly Father.

Our authority should be so tempered with kindness, meekness, and loving tenderness that our children may fear us with delight, and see that we love them with as much delight.) Now, let our authority effectually keep our children from all their unruly exorbitancies and extravagancies. If we let our young folks grow headstrong, and if we grow afraid of compelling them to the wholesome orders of our families, we have given them up to ruin. God brought that son to an untimely and terrible end, of whom it is reported in 1 Kings 1:6, "His father had not displeased him at any time, in saying, 'Why hast thou done so?' "

I beseech you, parents, interpose your authority to stop and check the carriage of your children when they are running into the paths of the destroyer) Gratify them with rewards of well doing when they do well, but do not let them be gratified with every ungodly vanity that their vain minds may be set upon. Keep a strict inspection upon their conversations; examine how they spend their time; examine what company they keep; examine whether they take any bad courses.

Do not be such foolish enemies to yourselves and your children as to count those as your enemies who advise you of your children's miscarriages. That wretched folly is a very frequent one! When you find out their miscarriages, effectually rebuke and restrain them. Do not incure the indigation of heaven that was once incurred by a fond father in 1 Samuel 3:13: "I will judge his house forever, for the iniquity which he knoweth; because his sons made themselves vile and he restrained them not."

Ah, you indulgent parent, if you cannot cross your children when they are disposed to that which is dishonoring to God, God will make your children to be crosses unto you. Sirs, when your children do amiss, call them aside; set before them the precepts of God which they have broken, and the threatenings of God which they have provoked. Demand of them that they profess their sorrow for their faults, and that they resolve that they will be so faulty no more.

Yea, there may be occasion for you to consider that word from God found in Proverbs 13:24: "He that spareth his rod hateth his son, but he that loveth him chasteneth him betimes." Add to that this word found in Proverbs 19:18: "Chasten thy son while there is hope, and let not thy soul spare for his crying." And Proverbs 23:13–14: "Withhold not correction from the child; for if thou beatest him with the rod, he shall not die. Thou shalt beat him with the rod, and shalt deliver his soul from hell." But if you must strike your child, remember this counsel: never give a blow in a passion; wait until your passion is over, and let the offenders plainly see that you deal thus with them out of pure obedience to God, and for their true repentance. One of the ancients had this ingenious insight: In the tabernacle, Aaron's rod and the pot of manna were together. So, when the rod is used, the sweetness and goodness of the manna must accompany it, and mercy must be joined with severity.

Let me leave this section with that wisdom from Proverbs 29;15: "A child left unto himself bringeth his mother to shame."

5. Lay your charges upon your children. Parents, charge them to work about their own salvation. The charges of parents have a great efficacy upon many children. To charge them vehemently is to charm them wonderfully. Command your children and, it may be, they will obey. Let God's commands be your commands and, it may be, your children will obey them. Lay upon

your children the charges of God, as David did once upon his, in 1 Chronicles 28:9: "My son, know thou the God of thy father, and serve Him with a perfect heart, and with a willing mind; if thou seek Him, He will be found of thee, but if thou forsake Him, He will cast thee off forever."

Sirs, you will do well to single out some singular charges of God. Call your children before you one by one and lay those charges upon them in the name of the God who made them. Obtain from your children, if you can, a promise that they will observe those charges with the help of God. I will set before you three or four of those charges.

Let one of your charges upon your children be that from 1 John 3:23: "This is His commandment, that we should believe on the name of His Son, Jesus Christ." Charge them to carry their poor, guilty, ignorant, polluted, and enslaved souls unto the Lord Jesus Christ, so that He may save them from their sins, and save them from the wrath to come. Charge them to mind how the Lord Jesus Christ executes the office of a prophet, a priest, and a king; and cry to Him that He would save them in the execution of all those blessed offices.

Let another of your charges be that one from Haggai 1:5: "Thus saith the Lord of Hosts, 'Consider your ways.' " Charge them to set apart a few minutes now and then for consideration, and in those minutes, charge them to consider what they have been doing, what they should have been doing ever since they came into the world, and if they should immediately go out of the world, what will become of them throughout eternal ages.

I have read of a dying parent who laid this charge

upon his wild son: that he would allow one quarter of an hour every day to consider something or other, any thing, as his fancy led him. The young man, having for some while done so, at last began to consider why his dying parent should lay such a charge upon him. This brought on so many devout thoughts that before long the desire of the dying parent was accomplished in the conversion of the young man.

Oh, if you could engage your children to think upon their ways, there would be hope of their turning to God.

But, let your third charge be that from Matthew 6:6: "Enter into thy closet, and when thou hast shut thy door, pray to thy Father that sees in secret." Charge them to retire for secret prayer every day. Talk with them till you see that they can tell what they should pray for. Then often charge them to pray every day; yea, sometimes ask them, "Do you remember the charge I laid upon you?"

Ah, parent, your children will do well as long as it can be said, "Behold, they pray." And your house filled with your children's prayers would be better accommodated than if it were filled with all the riches of the Indies.

Let your fourth charge be from Proverbs 9:6: "Forsake the foolish and live." Charge them to avoid the snares of evil company; terrify them with warnings of those deadly snares. Often repeat this charge unto them: if there is any vicious company, shun them as you would the plague or the devil. Often say, "My son, if sinners entice thee, consent thou not." Often say, "My child, walk with the wise and thou shalt be wise, but a companion of fools shall be destroyed."

Oh, do not let the beasts of prey carry away your children alive.

It is here intimated that an Abraham is to command his children very particularly about the way of the Lord. The way of the Lord is the way of His right, pure, instituted worship. Well, then, command your children to not forsake the holy institutions of the Lord Jesus Christ and embrace a vain worship, consisting of things that He never instituted. There are some clauses in the Second Commandment which intimate that if parents would see the mercies of God upon their children, they must charge them to worship God only in those ways of worship that God has appointed.

Thus keep charging your children while you live. And if you are capable of doing so, do it once more with all possible solemnity when you come to die. The words of a dying parent will probably be living words and lively ones.

When our excellent Mitchel was dying, he let fall such a speech as this unto a young gentleman who lodged in his house, "My friend, as a dying man I now charge you that you don't meet me out of Christ in the day of Christ." This one speech brought into Christ the soul of that young gentleman! Truly, if your dying lips may utter such dying words unto your children, who can tell but they may then be brought into Christ, if they were never so before!

But, lest you should have no opportunity to speak in a dying hour, why should you not write such things as you would have them to think upon when you shall be dead and gone? Your children may reap an unknown deal of good from the admonitions that a dying parent may leave unto them.

6. Parents, be exemplary. Your example may do much towards the salvation of your children; your works will more work upon your children than your words; your patterns will do more than your precepts, your copies more than your counsels.

What was then said unto pastors in Titus 2:7 may very fitly be said unto parents: "In all things show thyself a pattern of good works." And 1 Timothy 4:12: "Be thou an example in word, in conversation, in charity, in spirit, in faith, and in purity."

It will be impossible for you to infuse any good into your children if you appear void of that good yourselves. If the old crab goes backward, it is to no purpose for the young one to be directed to go forward. Sirs, young ones will crawl after the old ones.

Would you have your children well-principled with the fear and faith of God? Mind that passage in Acts 10:2: "Cornelius was a devout man, and one that feared God, with all his house." Mind that passage in Acts 18:8: "Crispus believed on the Lord, with all his house." It seems that the whole house is likely to do as the parents do. It is as Augustine expressed it, "We will be no better than our parents." If the parents will make their cakes to the queen of heaven, the children will kindle their fires for them.

Justin Martyr was once asked why the prophet Elisha imprecated the revenges of heaven upon the children who mocked him, when they hardly understood what they did. He answered that the children learned their wicked language from their parents, and now God punished both of them together.

Parents, let your children see nothing from you but what shall be commendable and imitable. Be able to say unto your children, "My child, follow me, as you have seen me follow Christ." From your seriousness, your prayerfulness, and your watchfulness, and your sanctification of the Lord's Day, let them be taught how they should walk and please God. You bid them well, now show them how!

7. Prayer must be the crown of all. Parents, is it your heart's desire that your children may be saved? Let it be also your prayer for your children that they may be saved. Prayer for the salvation of any sinners avails much. How much may it avail for the salvation of our sinful children? That prayer of David in 1 Chronicles 29:19 availed much: "Lord, give unto my son a perfect heart, to keep Thy commandments."

Parents, make such a prayer for your children: "Lord, give unto my child a new heart, a clean heart, a soft heart, and a heart after Thy own heart."

We have been told that children once were brought unto our Lord Jesus Christ, for Him to put His hands upon them. And He put His hands upon them and blessed them. Oh, three and four times blessed children! Well, parent, bring your children unto the Lord Jesus Christ; it may be that He will put His blessing, healing, and saving hands upon them. Then they are blessed, and shall be blessed forevermore! Abraham cried to God, "Oh, that my son Ishmael may live in Thy sight!" And God said to Abraham concerning Ishmael, "I have heard thee!"

Pray for the salvation of your children, and carry the names of every one of them every day before the Lord with prayers, the cries whereof shall pierce the very heavens. Job 1:5: "He [Job] offered according to the number of all his children; thus Job did continually."

Address heaven with daily prayers that God would make your children the temples of His Spirit, the vessels of His glory, and the care of His holy angels. Address the Lord Jesus Christ with prayers like those of old, that all the maladies upon the souls of your children may be cured, and that the evil one may have no possession of them.

Yea, when you cast your eyes upon the little folks, often in a day dart up an ejaculatory prayer to heaven for them: "Lord, let this child be Thy servant forever." If your prayers are not immediately answered, do not be disheartened. Remember the words of the Lord in Luke 18:1: "Men ought always to pray, and not to faint." Double your importunity until you succeed for your child, as the poor woman of Canaan did.

Join fasting to your prayer; it may be that the evil in the soul of your child will not go out without such a remedy. David set himself to fasting as well as prayer for the life of his child. Oh, do as much for the soul of your child! Wrestle with the Lord. Accept no denial. Earnestly protest, "Lord, I will not let Thee go unless Thou bless this poor child of mine and make it Thine own!" Do this until, if it may be, your heart is raised by a touch of heaven to a belief that God has blessed this child, and it shall be blessed and saved forever.

But is this all that is to be done? There is more. Parents, pray with your children as well as for them. Family prayer must be maintained by all those parents who would not have their children miss salvation, and who would not have the damnation of their children horribly fall upon themselves. Man, your family is a pagan family if it is a prayerless family. And the children going down to the place of dragons from your family will pour out their execrations upon you in the bottom of hell until the very heavens are no more.

But, besides your family prayers, O parents, why should you not now and then take one capable child after another alone before the Lord? Carry the child with you into your secret chambers; make the child kneel down by you while you present it unto the Lord, and implore His blessing upon it. Let the child hear the groans and see the tears, and be a witness of the agonies wherewith you are travailing for the salvation of it. The children will never forget what you do; it will have a marvelous force upon them.

Thus, O parents, you have been told what you have to do for the salvation of your children. And certainly their salvation is worth all of this! Your zeal about the salvation of your children will be a symptom of your own sincerity. A total want of zeal will be a spot upon you that is not a spot of the children of God. God will reward the zeal. It is very probable that the children thus cared for will be the saved by the Lord. Your glad hearts will one day see it, if they are so; it will augment your heaven through all eternity to have these in heaven with you.

And let it be remembered that the fathers are not the only parents obliged thus to pursue the salvation of their children. You who are mothers have more than a little to do for the souls of your children, and you have opportunity to do more than a little. Bathsheba, the mother of Solomon, and Eunice, the mother of Timothy, greatly contributed unto the salvation of their famous and worthy sons.

God has commanded children, "Forsake not the law of thy mother." Then a mother must give the law of

God unto them. It is said of the virtuous woman in Proverbs 31 that "She looks well to the ways of her household." Then a virtuous mother looks well to the ways of her children.

Your children may say, "In sin did my mother conceive me." Oh, then let mothers do what they can to save their children out of sin! And especially, mothers, travail for your children over again, with your earnest prayers for their salvation, until it may be said unto you as it was unto Monica, the mother of Augustine, concerning him, "It is impossible that your child should perish, after you have employed so many prayers and tears for his salvation."

Now may God give good success to these poor endeavors!

The Duties of Children to their Parents

"The Levites shall speak, and shall say unto all the men
of Israel with a loud voice, 'Cursed is he that setteth
light by his father or his mother.' And all the
people shall say, 'Amen.' "
Deuteronomy 27:14, 16

I am going to entertain you with a discourse that
cannot have a more fitting preface than those words in
Psalm 34:11: "Come, ye children; hearken unto me. I
will teach you the fear of the Lord." The children of my
neighbors are now appearing among us. Yea, our little
ones are no little part of this assembly. And very many
of these are the children of pious parents, the children
whose piety has therefore been fervently desired and
required by their parents. Come, ye children, hearken
to me. I will tell you what you shall do so that your parents may be happy in you, and that your own happiness
may be secured and increased.

There was a solemnity sometimes observed upon the
two mountains of Ebal and Gerizim in the land of
Israel. On the top of Mount Ebal there stood six of the
Israelitish tribes and six on the top of Mount Gerizim.
Certain Levites with the ark of God in the valley between them, directing themselves unto Mount Ebal
with a loud voice, uttered very distinctly no less than
twelve terrible curses, unto which the tribes on that
mount made the very heavens ring with a dreadful

23

"Amen" unto them. But between each of these curses, the Levites directed themselves unto Mount Gerizim with blessings directly opposed unto those curses; and the tribes on that mount gave the shout of a joyful "Amen" upon them.

It is true, the order prescribing the blessings is not so distinctly recited by Moses as that of the curses; because 'tis reserved as the special glory of our blessed Lord Jesus Christ, and of His glorious gospel, to bring in the blessings of obedience. Until the gospel of the Lord Jesus Christ arrives unto us, the law pronounces unto us nothing but curses; we hear nothing but a thunder of wrath cursing us.

The second of the direful curses which the Levites of God, facing Mount Ebal, pronounced was, "Cursed be he that sets light by his father or his mother." Doubtless, when the vast body of people, as one man, replied, "Amen," upon it, it sounded like a horrible thunderclap. Yea, but the thunderclap is not yet over; the peals of it are this very day to be again sounded in the midst of you, O congregation of God.

We read that when the thing thus appointed was first observed by the tribes of Israel in the days of Joshua (Joshua 8:35), there were little ones in the congregation. It is not amiss that there are so many little ones in this great congregation here come together, and unto them especially I am now to bring this warning from God: The heavy curse of God will fall upon those children who make light of their parents. To set light by one's parents is, in other words, to treat them with any ungodly contempt. You mind it, my children, the curse of God is not only denounced upon children who cast contempt upon their fathers. Oftentimes the fathers have the wisdom to keep up their authority, and keep themselves above the contempt of their children. But the mothers do more frequently, by their fondness and weakness, bring upon themselves the contempt of their children, and lay themselves low by many impertinencies.

Now, behold the admonition of heaven; (the children who cast contempt upon their mothers also bring themselves under the curse of God. The curse of God!) The most terrible thing that ever was heard of, the "first-born" of terrible things! Can I mention this tremendous thing, the curse of God, and, O my children, will you not tremble at it!

Who can forbear crying out, as Elihu did when he heard the thunders of God railing in the heavens over him, "At this my heart even trembles, and it is moved out of its place!" I hope, none of you have come to such a degree of atheism as to defy the curse of God. You won't mock at the fear of the most fearful thing in the world.

But give me your attention while, from the oracles of the almighty God, I handle this question for you.

QUESTION: What respect to their parents must be rendered by the children who would not, by affronts to their parents, bring down upon themselves the dreadful curses of God?

The answers, the lessons, which I have now to set before you, my children, are these:

Maintain in your own spirits a dread of those dreadful curses with which the God of heaven takes vengeance on the children who do not put respect, but rather contempt, upon their parents. How dreadfully the judgments of God follow the children who set light by their parents. And, oh, my warned children, upon the sight of those warnings, cry out, "Lord, my flesh trembles for fear, and I am afraid of those judgments!"

Indeed there is no sin more usually revenged by the sensible and notable curses of God than that sin of the contempt of parents. Exasperated parents themselves sometimes imprecate curses upon their children; and the invisible world, with a strange but a quick work, usually says, "Amen," to those curses.

But, I beseech you, O parents, let your exasperations be what they will, forbear to use any imprecations on your children. Alas, they will be cursed children fast enough without the least ill wish of yours to hasten it.

When it was instituted that the Levites were to proclaim, "Cursed is he that sets light by his father or his mother," one part of the institution was, "All the people shall say, 'Amen.' " Truly it often comes to pass that when the curses of God come upon those who set light by their parents, it shall be so that all the people shall take notice of it; all the people who shall see an "amen" set unto it shall see it ratified.

Children, I must be a little particular with you. Undutiful children, for the sin of the contempt they cast upon their parents, are often cursed by God with being left unto yet more sin against Him. I could not have spoken a more terrible word! This is most certain: the more sinful any man is, the more cursed is that man. It is an amazing vengeance of God that gives a sinner up to sin for sin, and curses a sinner for one sin by leaving him to another. But undutiful children are commonly cursed and banned by such a vengeance of God. We read of some sinners whom the justice of God gives up to sin, and this is one brand upon those doleful sinners from Romans 1:30, disobedient to parents.

The Fifth Commandment stands in the front of all six upon the second table of the law. Children, if you break the Fifth Commandment, there is not much likelihood that you will keep the rest. No, there is hazard that the curse of God will give you up to break every one of them.

Undutiful children soon become horrid creatures: unchaste, dishonest, lying, and all manner of abominations. And the contempt which they cast upon the advice of their parents is one thing that pulls down this curse of God upon them. They who sin against their parents are sometimes given up to sin by God against all the world beside. Mind the most scandalous instances of wickedness and villainy, and you'll ordinarily find that they were first undutiful children before they fell into the rest of their atrocious wickedness.

Undutiful children, for the contempt they cast upon their parents, are often cursed by God with a mischief brought upon all their affairs. A strange disaster usually follows undutiful children; much evil pursues that kind of sinner. There is a secret vengeance of God, perplexing their affairs; through that vengeance of God none of their affairs prosper with them. When David was vexed with one of his undutiful children, he could foretell (Psalm 55:19) that God would afflict them. There is a secret blast of God upon undutiful children.

If they are afflicted in their estates, it is the curse of God upon them for their being loathe to do what they could for their parents with their estates. If they are afflicted in their bodies, it is the curse of God upon them for their dishonoring the parents of their bodies.

If God afflicts them with reproaches, it is the curse

of God upon them for having reproached or despised their parents.

Perhaps they are followed with one plague after another by the irresistible wrath and curse of God; and they can't comprehend how they came to be so plagued in all their interests. It may be that it is their contempt of their parents that has been the worm at the root, which causes all to wither with them.

And if these undutiful children ever live to have children of their own, God pays them in their own coin. God pays them back with the undutifulness of their own children. God makes those children to possess the iniquities of the parents' youth.

Judah cast contempt upon his parents by marrying a Canaanitess, seemingly without their consent. God cursed this Judah with a couple of children who were such wretches that the immediate hand of heaven dispatched them out of the world.

You have doubtless been informed of that famous history in the *Theatrum Historie*. A vile son once beat his old father, and then dragged him to the threshold of the house by the hair of the head. Afterwards, when he grew old himself (which, by the way, was a rare thing) his own son beat him in like manner, and then dragged him also by the hair of the head not only to the threshold, but out of doors into the dirt. Hereupon he cried out with anguish, "Ah! If this varlet had pulled me only to the threshold, I would have been served just as my father was by me!" Children, remember this example.

A third curse of God upon undutiful children is death, and not a rare one for their being so. It is the tenor of the precept, "Honor thy father and thy mother, that thy days may be long upon the land." Mind it, children, your days are not likely to be long upon the land if you set light by your father or mother.

When Absalom, with his crew, was manifesting a bloody undutifulness, his offended father predicted that those bloody and crafty men would not live out half their days. Why? Because he knew that the very finger of God had once written that children who do not honor their parents must not look to have their days long in the land.

We have all heard the fate of that undutiful Absalom. Some travellers recently reported that in the place where Absalom was buried, there is now a vast heap of stones. It is customary for those who go by the place to throw a stone upon it, using these words: "Thus it shall be done unto the son who rebels against his father."

Stand still, O my children, and look with horror upon the grave of Absalom. Read there and see the curse of God upon the undutiful. Children who cast contempt on the parents, who have been the instruments of giving them life, thereby do what but make forfeitures of their Life?

It becomes children to reckon it one main design, business, and privilege of their life to be comforts unto their parents. When they cease to do so, God, with a direful curse, often gives that order concerning them, "Take away the life of that undutiful creature! That creature shall no longer live in the world." It was an edict of heaven in Exodus 21:17: "He that curseth his father or his mother shall surely be put unto death."

And what shall then be done unto the children who prove to be curses unto their fathers or their mothers?

Undutiful children are so; but the curse of God may put
them to death for it. And because those undutiful children are overly wicked, therefore they die before their
time. Yea, 'tis no unusual thing for the death of undutiful children to be embittered with some extraordinary
circumstances of confusion and calamity. I tell you, O
undutiful children, there is danger of you being so
cursed of God as to be hanged on a tree at the end.

It is remarkable that most who are executed on the
gallows at their execution cry out something like this:
"Oh, 'tis my undutifulness unto my parents, my disobe-
dience unto my parents, that has brought me unto this
lamentable end!" It is a memorable passage that we
find in Proverbs 30:17: "The eye that mocks at his father, and despises to obey his mother, the ravens of the
valley shall pick it out, and the young eagles shall eat
it." It seems that an untimely and tragic death often ex-
poses the carcasses of those children to the carnivorous
fowls of heaven.

There was a law in Israel (Deuteronomy 21:21) that
the rebellious child should be put to death. After ston-
ing he was hung, for in Israel they hung none till they
had first otherwise killed him; and no doubt, his corpse
being taken down, as it was to be done before sunset, it
was thrown into a pit, such a one as that into which
they threw the corpse of Judas over the precipice, and
there the fowls of heaven preyed upon it. Agur is perhaps alluding to this in Proverbs 30:17. And we often
see that the rebellious child is left by God unto those
crimes for which he is put to death before long.

More than this, undutiful children are unnatural
children. And the curse of God sometimes gives over
unnatural children to commit the most unnatural

murders. They have murdered themselves, and been self-destroyers; and as they have sinned against nature, so they die the most against nature that can be.

A young man in this country drowned himself, but he left behind him a writing to his father wherein he complained, "O father, I have kept my soul as long as I could. My ruin was the pride and stubbornness of my tender years!"

But is this all? No, lastly, all the curse of God upon undutiful children hitherto is but death riding the pale horse seen in Revelation, whereof 'tis said, "Hell followed." I am here to tell you that the vengeance of eternal fire will be the portion of undutiful children after all. Children who cast contempt upon their parents will be cast by God into the vengeance of eternal fire at last, and into everlasting contempt.

Surely the damned are the cursed of God! Hear, O children, if you are the children of rebellion, the curse of God will make you the children of perdition throughout eternal ages. What are undutiful children but the children of Belial? This is as much as to say that they are the children of Satan; and unto Satan they shall go. The Bible has called them "the children of the devil," and where shall the children of the devil go but into the everlasting fire prepared for the devil and his angels? The fiends of darkness will be the ravens and the eagles that shall fasten their talons in the eyes of those children.

When our Lord Jesus Christ, the Judge of the world, foretells that, on the day of judgment, having said unto those on His right hand, "Come ye blessed," He will say unto those on His left hand, "Depart, ye cursed, into everlasting fire, with the devil and his angels," He

seems to allude to the action between Gerizim and
Ebal. Truly, the children damned of old upon Mount
Ebal, for setting light by their fathers or their mothers,
will be they whom the Lord Jesus Christ will one day
doom to depart from Him into everlasting fire with the
devil and his angels. It was said in Proverbs 20:20:
"Whoso curseth his father or his mother, his lamp
shall be put out in obscure darkness." Children, if by
undutifulness to your parents you incur the curse of
God, it won't be long before you go down into obscure
darkness, even into utter darkness. God has reserved for
you the blackness of darkness forever. Be it known to
you that undutifulness to your parents will bring you to
feel many stripes from an enraged conscience in the
world to come. You know the will of God, and your undutifulness is a sin against your conscience.

Yea, be dutiful to your parents, or expect all the
formidable outpourings of an infinite and eternal
wrath upon your soul. You do not value the wrath of
your parents; it is a light thing to you. But the wrath of
the Lord God Omnipotent, oh, don't make light of
that! It is a fearful thing to fall into the hands of the living God!

I hope that we have been long enough upon Mount
Ebal. Shall we now turn a little unto Mount Gerizim?

Let the signal blessings of God upon children who
treat their parents with due respect find much respect
with you, be a great encouragement unto you, and have
a strong impression upon you. The Levites, as far as we
understand, were to turn unto Mount Gerizim and with
a loud voice were to say, "Blessed be he who doth not
set light by his father or his mother." And all the
people were to say, "Amen." Hearken, O my children, to

the blessings of God that shall be poured and showered from on high upon the dutiful; and let them charm you into all possible dutifulness.

There are children whose continual desire and prayer it is that they may be in all things made rich blessings unto their parents. They honor their parents, and are an honor to their parents. Their parents, with glad hearts, behold their wisdom, and must bear this testimony for them: Never were parents more happy in their children.

Oh, the blessings that belong to children of such a character! If it might be said (as it was by David, when God gave him a dutiful son to build the temple of the Lord in Psalm 127:5), "Blessed is the man that hath his quiver full of such arrows," then surely it can be said, "Blessed are the arrows that are in the quiver of such a man!"

The Holy Spirit of God sets a special remark upon that command which requires children to be dutiful unto their parents. Ephesians 6:3 says that it is the first command [of the second table] with a promise: "That it may be well with thee."

It shall be well with you, O you dutiful children; you have the Word of God for it. You may note that in the command what we translate, "that thy days may be long," is to be read, "that they may prolong thy days." Who is this "they?" They are your father and your mother. But how can your father and your mother prolong your days? How but by blessing you in the name of Almighty God.

If the days of such a child are not prolonged, we must allow a sovereignty in such dispensations of heaven; but there is cause to hope for such a child that

God has prolonged his days in the happiness of the
heavenly Word.

This is plain: those parents who are blessed with dutiful children do, with an inexpressible agony, wish all
sorts of blessings to their children. If it were in their
power to confer blessings upon their children, oh, how
much they would do for them!

Now, because it is in the power of God alone to confer blessings upon us, these parents go to God for their
children, and they say with good old Jacob, "God bless
the lads!"

I assure you, such benedictions from obliged parents have a more than ordinary authority and efficacy
in them. For one's parents to go before God and plead,
"Ah, Lord, such a child of mine has loved me, served
me, and helped me; and his good carriage to me has
been such that even upon that account I have reason to
wish him all the good in the world. I therefore bring
that child unto Thee, and I pray Thee to bless him with
all blessings of goodness." To be thus blessed by one's
parents, O my children, is a thing of more value than if
a rich inheritance were to be received from them.

This is very certain: there is no point of religion,
more certainly and commonly rewarded with blessings
in this world than that of rendering unto parents the
dues that pertain unto them. A signal prosperity, even
in this world, usually attends those children who are
very obedient or serviceable unto their parents. To
those who obey the commandment of their father, thus
said the Lord of Hosts, "They shall stand before Me forever."

There are children who have with unspeakable
pleasure supported their aged parents in their necessi-

ties. They have said unto their needy parents, like
Joseph, "Thus saith thy son, 'Come down to me, Thou
shalt be near to me!' "

I believe that there are some at this very time, in this
very place, who can say that from the time they did for
their parents as they have done, God has signally
smiled upon them. Friend, that aged father or mother
in your house is not only the glory of your house, but a
better and richer thing than a mine of silver there.

Children, be blessings to your parents, and be as-
sured that those parents will be greater blessings to you
than you can be to them. They will be so as long as they
live; yea, more than so. After your parents are dead and
gone, the effects of their prayers will yet live. All the
prayers which those gratified parents put up for you will
be still answering after they are dead, as long as you
yourselves do live.

David had been a son, very tender of his parents:
and now he says in Psalm 27:10, "When my father and
my mother forsake me, then the Lord will take me up."
In other words, "He'll requite all that I did for my father
and my mother."

Shall I go a step further? When you yourselves also
are dead and gone, even your children may reap the
fruits of what you did for your parents. Your posterity
may fare the better for your dutifulness.

The Jews have a notion among them that for the
sake of the honor that Esau paid unto his father, the
Israelites long after might not extirpate the Edomites,
who were the posterity of Esau.

Moses told the Israelites, "You have compassed this
mountain long enough." Why? Because Esau compassed a mountain in hunting for his father.

Having said all this, dutiful children, acting upon
principles of Christianity, may hope to meet with their
Christian parents in heaven. There Abraham the reli-
gious father, Isaac the dutiful son, and Jacob the dutiful
grandson, are together. Blessed are they who meet
there in the light of the face of God. Blessed throughout eternal ages! Consider this, O children; and do not
set light by your parents.

But being prepared by these considerations, it may
now be time to say that the respects that children must
render unto their parents are comprised in these three
words: reverence, obedience, and recompence. Children set light by their parents, or cast contempt on
them, if they withhold any of these three regards from
them, and the curse of God will revenge the contempt.

Reverence
First, you set light by your parents if you withhold
from them the reverence that is due unto them.

The God of nature has placed a distance between
parents and their children. Children then set light by
their parents when they forget this distance.

There is first an inward reverence that children owe
unto their parents. It was enjoined in Leviticus 19:3: "Ye
shall fear every man his mother and his father."
Children, you set light by your parents if your minds are
not struck with some awful apprehension of their superiority over you, if you don't see an awful image of God
in their superiority, if you don't look upon them as the
very deputies of God in their several families.

But this reverence must have some outward expression given of it. There is an outward reverence that
children owe unto their parents. Hence it is said in

Malachi 1:6: "If I be a Father, where is My honor?" Hence it is said in Proverbs 31:28: "Her children rise up and call her blessed."

Their speeches, both *to* their parents and *of* their parents, must be full of reverence. When children speak *to* their parents, their language must carry in it some acknowledgment of their being such. Thus in Genesis 31:35: "She said unto her father, 'My Lord.' " When children speak *of* their parents, they must show a concern that nothing abusive be uttered. Thus in Psalm 127:5 the children of youth seem to defend their father from the enemies in the gate, or the false accusers.

And their actions towards their parents must yet more emphatically speak the reverence which they would retain for them. Thus in Genesis 48:12, Joseph bowed himself, with his face to the earth, before his father. Thus in I Kings 2:19, Solomon rose up to meet his mother, and bowed himself unto her, and she sat at his right hand.

Now, children, you set light by your parents if you talk sassily and clownishly unto them; if you reproach them, defame them, and backbite them; if your behavior towards them has any malapert impudence in it.

Though your parents may give you never so much occasion to complain, it becomes you to make as little reflection upon it as ever you can. Say nothing but what the glory of God makes it necessary for you to say. Though they should happen to do you any injuries, you may not show those resentments that you have upon the injuries of other persons.

Obedience

You set light by your parents if you withhold from them the obedience that is due unto them. If children don't study to do what their parents would have them to do, and if the word and will of their parents do not have the force of a law upon them, the children set light by them in such a misbehavior.

It was demanded in Ephesians 6:1: "Children, obey your parents in the Lord, for this is right." Children, you set light by your parents if you don't count it a right, just, fair, and very reasonable thing for you to be the servants of those who have done so much for you, their children; and beware of crossing those who have done so much to comfort you.

Colossians 3:20: "Children, obey your parents in all things, for this is well-pleasing unto the Lord." But, children, you set light by your parents if it is not also very well-pleasing unto you to please them, so far as without sin you may do so, and if you are not unwilling at any time to give them any displeasure.

When the father of Joseph laid his commands upon him, he obeyed those commands, though at the risk of his very life. It should be the very joy of your life to yield obedience unto the commands of your parents. Do your parents give you any instruction? You are called upon, in Proverbs 4:1 to "Hear, ye children, the instruction of a father." Most of all, in the grand motions and changes of your life, children, your parents are to be consulted, and the satisfaction of your parents is to be proposed.

In your callings, and in your matches especially, the directions of your parents must be of exceeding moment with you. Indeed, nothing should be done without them! Wherefore, children, you set light by your parents if you make nothing of their commands, and if you tread their just reproofs under foot.

You set light by them if you leave undone what they desire, and, much more, if you do what they forbid.

You set light by them if their anger is a light matter with you.

Recompence

You set light by your parents if you withhold from them the recompence that is due unto them.

Those children evidently set light by their parents who are insensible of the obligations which their parents have laid upon them, or who count anything too much to be done by children for their parents.

Of Joseph it is said in Genesis 47:12: "He nourished his father, and all his father's household with bread." And it is elsewhere pressed upon us, "Despise not thy mother when she is old." Children, you set light by your parents if you don't requite them as well as you can, and if you imagine that you can ever requite them enough.

It was a sad saying of Luther's that one father will more willingly maintain ten sons than ten sons will maintain one father. But those children set light by their parents who would not as willingly maintain their father as maintain their children, and who would not gladly be to their mother the restorer of her life, and the nourisher of her old age, as the mother of Ruth found her son-in-law to be unto her.

It was demanded in 1 Timothy 5:4: "Let the children learn to show piety at home, and requite their parents; for that is good and acceptable before God." Those children have no piety in them, they set light by God as well as by their parents, unto whom it is not a most acceptable thing to make some recompence unto their parents for all the vast benefits which their parents have heaped upon them.

Children, do you think that you can ever make recompence unto those who have borne you, bred you, fed you, and endured thousands of sorrows for you?

One says, "Many treat their parents as they do their candles: they set them in high candlesticks while they are full of tallow, but when all their substance is wasted they tread them underfoot."

And there are some who do not support their parents, but wrong them, rob them, and pillage them. They waste their parents.

Alas, children, you set light by your parents in all of this impiety. But, oh, don't make light of this impiety. Say, "Destruction from God is a terror to me!"

By father and mother, all sorts of parents are intended. Let the caution be accordingly extended, and set light by no sorts of parents whatsoever. Natural parents cannot safely come under the contempt of the children. God will curse the children who set light by them. And can you dream, then, that God will allow any contempt of political parents, of ecclesiastical or scholastic parents? There are parents in the commonwealth as well as in the family; there are parents in the church, and parents in the school, as well as in the commonwealth. If you set light by these parents, you herd yourselves among the cursed of God.

Remember, O servants, your master is your father and your mistress is your mother. Do not set light by your master or your mistress lest the curse of God at last hang upon you in chains, among the monuments of His indignation. Because your superiors in the family are your parents, therefore there is laid that charge of God upon you in 1 Peter 2:18 "Servants, be subject unto your masters with all fear, not only to the good and gentle, but also to the froward."

The proud hearts of many servants make them discontent in their servile state; the subjection expected from them throws them into a very grumbling discontent. You proud wretches, your sin was the very sin that at first made all the devils in hell! The devils, those proud spirits, could not bear to be servants in such a station as God had ordered for them; and for their pride, the Almighty has cursed and damned them. Servants, have a care lest by your pride you fall into the condemnation of the devil. It is the providence and the ordinance of the Lord Jesus Christ that has made you servants; and if, out of regard for Him, you carry well in your servitude, He will graciously accept all that you do as if it were done unto Himself. Colossians 3:23–24: "Servants, whatever ye do, do it heartily as unto the Lord, and not unto men; knowing that of the Lord you shall receive the reward of the inheritance [which belongs unto sons], for ye serve the Lord Christ." Well, then, don't set light by your masters. If they are masters, where is your fear of them? Do not expose their failings, if you see any in them. Let there be no sullenness, no sauciness, no rude retortings in your deportments towards them. Give them no cause to complain, as did Job, "I called my servant, and he gave me no answer."

Do not be those eye-servants who will do their

master's will no longer than their master's eye is upon
them. The all-seeing eye of the Almighty God is upon
you. Do not transgress their just commands either will-
fully or carelessly. If you do, the commands of God are
also transgressed in your miscarriages. Indeed, if your
masters bid you do an ill thing, you must with modest
expostulations suffer rather than obey. But if they bid
you do what is fitting and right, you sin against God if
you do it not. If they will not obey you, masters, turn
them out of doors.

Nor is this all that servants have to do. Servants, you
must use all diligence and faithfulness in your master's
business. A slothful servant is truly called a wicked servant. But Eleazer, the servant of Abraham, would not eat
his victuals till his master's business was dispatched.
Let your master's business be honestly discharged,
though you should, like Jacob, when a servant, have
your sleep departing from your eyes.

When your masters send you on errands, do not loi-
ter. Do not be sluggards to those who feed you. And be
the true sons of Israel, able to say, "Thy servants are true
men." Gehazi was a servant who lied unto his master,
but God made that liar to become a leper. Of all faults
in your servants, I advise you, masters, never let that of
lying go unpunished.

But that fault of stealing often accompanies it, of
which, O servants, beware; for God will never let that go
unpunished. I vehemently call upon you, never venture
to wrong your masters even for the value of a penny as
long as you live. Mark it, you'll entail eternal vexations
upon you, and God will make you lose a pound for every
penny whereof you have wronged your masters.

Have you ever purloined from them? Oh, fly penitently unto the blood of the Lord Jesus Christ for pardon, and make as much restitution, and as full reparation, as ever you can; or the jealous God will never pardon you till the torments of the damned have exacted the utmost farthing from you.

Servants, be such a blessing in your master's house as Joseph was to his. Contrive all the ways imaginable that your master may be the better for employing you. It may be that your master will bless God for you. However, God will bless you in your serving him. If you slight all these things, look for the curses of God.

And now, let people remember that rulers are parents. Don't set light by them. The charge of God upon people is that found in Titus 3:1–2: "Be subject . . . obey magistrates, be ready for every good work, and speak evil of no man [much less of magistrates]." Our setting light by excellent magistrates has been the scandalous crime of our country, and for that crime whole colonies may come to smart under the revenge of God.

Let churches remember that pastors are parents. Don't set light by them. The charge of God upon churches is found in Hebrews 13:17: "Obey them that have the rule over you, and submit yourselves; for they keep watch over your souls, as they that must give account; let them do it with joy, and not with grief, for that is unprofitable for you."

There has been a disorder called "Korahism," sometimes very extravagant. But for setting light by ministers who have been holy, able, faithful, and painful men of God, God sometimes removes a candlestick out of its place, or at least says, "Never shall a burning and a shining light be seen standing in it again."

Let scholars regard their tutors as their parents. My

child, the master of the school is a father to you. Those
who were under the education of Moses are called "the
sons of Moses." Wherefore, scholars, with all conscience of God, honor your tutors, and perform the
tasks which they impose upon you. Don't set light by
your schoolmaster, but love him, prize him, hearken to
him, and be thankful to him, and thankful to God for
him. These are ways to escape the curses of God.

They who have at any time set light by their parents
must go to God in Christ for His pardons so that His
curses may not overtake them. Who is there who can
say with the son in the gospel, who said unto his father,
"Lo, these many years I have served you, neither transgressed I at any time thy commandment?" The most dutiful child among us has been so defective in his dutifulness that he dares not plead it before God in his jus-
tification. He must say, as in Psalm 143:2, "Lord, enter
not into judgment with Thy servant; for in Thy sight
shall no man living be justified."

What then shall we do? Why, we read concerning
Mount Ebal, where the curses of God were fulminated
in Deuteronomy 27:5–7: "It was commanded, 'In Mount
Ebal, thou shalt build an altar unto the Lord thy God,
and thou shalt offer burnt offerings thereon unto the
Lord thy God, and thou shalt offer peace-offerings, and
rejoice before the Lord thy God.' " And we find that
Joshua afterwards did accordingly.

It is an ingenious note one commentator had upon
this passage: "This was no more than needed, for the
maledictions had no sooner been uttered but condemnation and execution instantly ensued, if these sacri-
fices with the merit of Christ therein typified had not
seasonably interceded."

Children, you hear the convex of heaven resounding from Ebal with the denunciations of God, "Cursed is he that sets light by his father or his mother." Our consciences tell us that we have done it many a time. Away, then, away to the antitype of the altar on Ebal. Oh, plead with God the burnt offering of Christ, and the peace-offering of Christ, that the curse of God may not seize upon us, that we may not be burnt in the flames of His indignation, and that He may be at peace with us forever.

When it was denounced, "Cursed is he that sets light by his father or his mother," it followed that all the people said, "Amen." "Amen" is the very name of Christ. May all the people now fly to that "Amen" so that they may be sheltered from the curses of God.

And, oh, call to mind the example of the Lord Jesus Christ. There never was in the world so dutiful a Son as He! We read in Luke 2:51 that He went down with His mother, and His reputed father, and though they were very low in the world, He became subject unto them. We read in John 19:27 that when He was in His last agonies, it lay very near His heart that His widowed mother might be provided for. He said unto a disciple, "Behold, thy Mother!" intimating that He would have him take her home unto his own house.

Now, though your dutifulness to your parents be never so complete, let this righteousness of the Lord Jesus Christ be all that you will plead with God as your title to the promised blessings of the dutiful.

Do not go on, children, if you value your lives and souls, do not go on to grieve your parents by any disrespect unto their admonitions, or by any vanity whatsoever. You cannot more make light of your parents than when you make light of their counsels: Your contempt of their counsels will speedily bring down God's curses upon you.

Moses did well when he hearkened unto the voice of his father-in-law, and did all that he had said. It is the voice of heaven in Proverbs 1:8: "My Son, hear the instruction of thy father, and forsake not the law of thy mother." Is it not the instruction of your father that you should avoid all vicious company, that you should pray in secret every day, that you should read and hear the Word of God with diligence? Or, if not so, it may be the law of your mother who is in travailing pains to see Christ formed in you.

Now, don't make light of the admonitions with which your parents are thus calling you. If your parents enjoin upon you anything that is not sinful, it will be a sin for you to refuse to do it. How much more is the sin if you refuse to do what the great God has first commanded, and your parents enjoin because the great God has first commanded?

Oh, my children, I am afraid that there are some of you who may read your doom in those ominous words found in 1 Samuel 2:25: "They hearkened not unto the voice of their father, because the Lord would slay them."

It is an unutterable grief that some of you give unto your pious parents. They see that you are still poor, carnal, and thoughtless creatures, and that perhaps a piece of fancy attire is of more account with you than Christ or your soul.

It is told to your parents that the ungodly youths in the town horribly poison one another. These youths cry up an indifference in religion, and say, "It is out of fashion for a man to be of one religion more than another. In reality they are saying that it is out of fashion to be of any religion at all. So they insensibly draw one another on to deride seriousness in religion, and the most serious and lively preachers of it, until they become idle, profane, sottish debauchees, and are soon ripe for the fiery indignation of God.

Your parents are trembling with an unknown distress and anguish lest you be entangled in a familiarity with these ungodly youths. It fills your parents with a grievous horror that they cannot see the marks of a regenerate soul upon you. They never hear you let fall a word that may reveal in you the least care of a never-dying soul. They cannot find out that there are any transactions between the Lord Jesus and you about the salvation of a soul in the hands of the destroyer.

As Augustine said of his blessed mother, so it may be said perhaps of yours, "She never saw me sinning against God but it brought the anguish of a new travail upon her."

It may be that you once had some good beginnings in religion. Your parents felt their hearts within them leap for joy at those beginnings. They hoped, "This my child was lost but is found, was dead but is alive!" But seeing that all your goodness is gone like the morning cloud and the early dew throws them into an extreme consternation.

How cheerfully would they give all they have in the world if they might say of you, "Behold, they pray!" They are every day extremely uneasy lest you die before you are born again, and it would have been good for you that you never had been born at all.

Ah, vain children, give some relief to this grief of

your parents. Fall down before the Lord and say, "Lord, Thou shalt be my Father, and the Guide of my youth." Turn to God in Christ, and become devout children. Then your parents shall say, "My heart, O my children, shall rejoice, even my heart!" But your parents feel that you make light of them so long as you lightly esteem the Rock of your Salvation, and make light of God, Christ, and the covenant of grace.

And now, I earnestly testify unto you that if you go on to sin against God and against your parents, the curses of the great God are impending over you. Those curses will horribly wound the head of those who go on still in their trespasses.

Yea, though you are the children of pious parents, the advantage you might have had by that shall be changed into a misery. The more pious parents you have had, the more forlorn children you shall be throughout eternal ages. We read that even the children of Abraham themselves will be cast into the fire of the wrath of God if they do not bring forth good fruit before Him. And we read of such among the damned as cry out, "Oh, Father Abraham, I am tormented in this flame!"

I read a story lately published about the famous Dr. [William] Twisse. He had been a very wicked boy. A schoolfellow of his died who was more wicked than he. The ghost of the dead lad appeared unto Twisse and horribly cried out, "I am damned!" This was, as Twisse's worthy son assures us, the occasion of Twisse's conversion unto God.

Oh, it is to be feared that many of our young people, after the madness of that ungodly life by which they broke the hearts of their parents, who have died at home and abroad, have gone unto the dead, if they could, in the form of a ghost, now appear unto their fellow sinners yet surviving, they would horribly cry out, "I am damned! I am damned for my ungodliness!"

But you have enough to warn you against all ungodliness without one coming to you from the dead. And while we thus warn you, there is this terrible intimation to be added unto all the rest: refractory child, your pious parents themselves will not own you in the day when God shall curse you, cut you off, and cast you out forever. And all the grief which your pious parents here endured for you and from you will be oil to the everlasting flames of that grief which you shall endure in the place of dragons.

Oh, come to a right mind, you prodigal, and by repentance give unto your pious parents cause to say, "This is a dear son, and a pleasant child." Then the God of heaven Himself will bless you and say, "I will surely have mercy upon them."

Sirs, a little book to assist in the education of children is now in your hands. But can they be well educated if their parents never send them to school? This is a point that seems now to call for some inculcation.

A good school deserves to be called the very salt of the town that has it. And the pastors of every town are under peculiar obligations to make it a part of their pastoral care, that they may have a good school in their neighborhood.

A woeful putrefaction threatens the rising generation. Barbarous ignorance, and the unavoidable consequence of it, outrageous wickedness, will make the rising generation loathsome if it does not have schools to preserve it.

Schools wherein the youth may, by able masters, be taught the things that are necessary to qualify them for future serviceableness, and have their manners therewithal well-formed under a laudable discipline, and be over and above well-catechised in the principles of religion, those would be a glory of our land, and the preservatives of all other glory.

The minister who shall give his neighbors no rest until they have agreeable schools among them, and who shall himself also at some times inspect and visit the schools, will therein do much towards fulfilling that part of his ministry, "Feed My lambs"; and his neighbors under his charge will (whatever they think of it) have cause to bless God for this expression of his faithfulness. But these are not the only persons to whom this matter belongs. The civil authority, and the whole vicinity, cannot be true to their own interest if they do not say, "We also will be with you."

When the Reformation began in Europe a hundred and fourscore years ago, to erect schools everywhere was one principal concern of the glorious and heroic reformers. And it was a common thing even for little villages of twenty or thirty families, in the midst of all their charges and their dangers, to maintain one of them.

The colonies of New England were planted on the design of pursuing that holy Reformation; and now the devil cannot give a greater blow to the Reformation among us than by causing schools to languish under discouragements.

If our general courts decline to contrive and provide laws for the support of schools, or if particular towns employ their wits for cheats to elude the wholesome laws, little do they consider how much they expose themselves to that rebuke of God, "Thou hast destroyed thyself, O New England."

Would we read in the ancient histories how zealous the more discreet pagans were to maintain schools among them, it might put us Christians to the blush, among whom 'tis common for schools to starve and sink. And a mind sordidly covetous withholds more than is meet, but it tends unto what is infinitely worse than poverty.

Sirs, what will be the issue of these things? The issue will be that if the church desires pastors more easily ordained, they will find such pastors—as the government has twisters of the law for lawyers, as medicine has beggars for physicians, as deceivers offer themselves for teachers.

But lest, through the want of schools, there should in a little while be scarcely one man in a place able to construe this description of the fate following upon that want, I will transcribe in plain English the first article of the *Prognostications Upon the Future State of New England*, lately published:

> Where schools are not vigorously and honorably encouraged, whole colonies will sink apace; into a degenerate and contemptible condition, and at last become horribly barbarous. And the first instance of their barbarity will be that they will be undone for want of men, but not see and own what it was that undid them.

You will therefore pardon my freedom with you if I
address you in the words of Luther:

> If ever there be any considerable blow given to
> the devil's kingdom, it must be by youth excellently
> educated. It is a serious thing, a weighty thing, and
> a thing that hath much of the interest of Christ, and
> of Christianity in it, that youth be well-trained up,
> and that schools, and school-masters be main-
> tained. Learning is an unwelcome guest to the
> devil, and therefore he would fain starve it out.
>
> But we shall never long retain the gospel without
> the help of learning. And if we should have no re-
> gard unto religion, even the outward prosperity of a
> people in this world would necessarily require
> schools and learned men. Alas, that none are car-
> ried with alacrity and seriousness to take care for
> the education of youth and to help the world with
> eminent and able men.

But the freedom with which this address is made
unto you is not so great as the fervor that has animated
it. My fathers and brethren, if you have any love to God
and Christ and posterity; let schools be more encour-
aged.

If you would not betray your posterity into the very
circumstances of savages, let schools have more encouragement. But in the anguish, the despair of success to be otherwise found by this address, I will turn it
from you unto the almighty Hearer of prayer.

"And, O Thou Savior and Shepherd of Thy New-
English Israel, be entreated mercifully to look down
upon Thy flocks in the wilderness. Oh, give us not up
to the blindness and madness of neglecting the lambs
in the flocks. Inspire Thy people, and all orders of men

among Thy people, with a just care for the education of posterity. Let well-ordered, well-instructed, and well-maintained schools be the honor and the defense of our land. Let learning, and all the helps and means of it, be precious in our esteem. And by learning let the interests of Thy gospel so prevail that we may be made wise unto salvation. Save us, O our Lord Jesus Christ. Save us from the mischiefs and scandals of an uncultivated offspring. Let this be a land of light unto Thee, O Sun of Righteousness; arise unto the world with healing in Thy wings. Amen."